aJournals

At aJournals, we recognise that a journal is a personal space where you have the opportunity to express yourself comfortably and honestly, no matter what the topic.
Each journal we have made is envisioned and conceived with a practical design to minimalize stress, help with organisation, and to inspire creativity.

For the good, the bad, and all the days in between.

www.a-journals.com

DATE:

LOCATION:

TIME:

TYPE:

HEIGHT:

DESCRIPTION:

SKETCH:

DATE:

LOCATION:

TIME:

TYPE:

HEIGHT:

DESCRIPTION:

SKETCH:

DATE:

LOCATION:

TIME:

TYPE:

HEIGHT:

DESCRIPTION:

SKETCH:

DATE:

LOCATION:

TIME:

TYPE:

HEIGHT:

DESCRIPTION:

SKETCH:

DATE:

LOCATION:

TIME:

TYPE:

HEIGHT:

DESCRIPTION:

SKETCH:

DATE:

LOCATION:

TIME:

TYPE:

HEIGHT:

DESCRIPTION:

SKETCH:

DATE:

LOCATION:

TIME:

TYPE:

HEIGHT:

DESCRIPTION:

SKETCH:

DATE:

LOCATION:

TIME:

TYPE:

HEIGHT:

DESCRIPTION:

SKETCH:

DATE:

LOCATION:

TIME:

TYPE:

HEIGHT:

DESCRIPTION:

SKETCH:

DATE:

LOCATION:

TIME:

TYPE:

HEIGHT:

DESCRIPTION:

SKETCH:

DATE:

LOCATION:

TIME:

TYPE:

HEIGHT:

DESCRIPTION:

SKETCH:

DATE:

LOCATION:

TIME:

TYPE:

HEIGHT:

DESCRIPTION:

SKETCH:

DATE:

LOCATION:

TIME:

TYPE:

HEIGHT:

DESCRIPTION:

SKETCH:

DATE:

LOCATION:

TIME:

TYPE:

HEIGHT:

DESCRIPTION:

SKETCH:

DATE:

LOCATION:

TIME:

TYPE:

HEIGHT:

DESCRIPTION:

SKETCH:

DATE:

LOCATION:

TIME:

TYPE:

HEIGHT:

DESCRIPTION:

SKETCH:

DATE:

LOCATION:

TIME:

TYPE:

HEIGHT:

DESCRIPTION:

SKETCH:

DATE:

LOCATION:

TIME:

TYPE:

HEIGHT:

DESCRIPTION:

SKETCH:

DATE:

LOCATION:

TIME:

TYPE:

HEIGHT:

DESCRIPTION:

SKETCH:

DATE:

LOCATION:

TIME:

TYPE:

HEIGHT:

DESCRIPTION:

SKETCH:

DATE:

LOCATION:

TIME:

TYPE:

HEIGHT:

DESCRIPTION:

SKETCH:

DATE:

LOCATION:

TIME:

TYPE:

HEIGHT:

DESCRIPTION:

SKETCH:

DATE:

LOCATION:

TIME:

TYPE:

HEIGHT:

DESCRIPTION:

SKETCH:

DATE:

LOCATION:

TIME:

TYPE:

HEIGHT:

DESCRIPTION:

SKETCH:

DATE:

LOCATION:

TIME:

TYPE:

HEIGHT:

DESCRIPTION:

SKETCH:

DATE:

LOCATION:

TIME:

TYPE:

HEIGHT:

DESCRIPTION:

SKETCH:

DATE:

LOCATION:

TIME:

TYPE:

HEIGHT:

DESCRIPTION:

SKETCH:

DATE:

LOCATION:

TIME:

TYPE:

HEIGHT:

DESCRIPTION:

SKETCH:

DATE:

LOCATION:

TIME:

TYPE:

HEIGHT:

DESCRIPTION:

SKETCH:

DATE:

LOCATION:

TIME:

TYPE:

HEIGHT:

DESCRIPTION:

SKETCH:

DATE:

LOCATION:

TIME:

TYPE:

HEIGHT:

DESCRIPTION:

SKETCH:

DATE:

LOCATION:

TIME:

TYPE:

HEIGHT:

DESCRIPTION:

SKETCH:

DATE:

LOCATION:

TIME:

TYPE:

HEIGHT:

DESCRIPTION:

SKETCH:

DATE:

LOCATION:

TIME:

TYPE:

HEIGHT:

DESCRIPTION:

SKETCH:

DATE:

LOCATION:

TIME:

TYPE:

HEIGHT:

DESCRIPTION:

SKETCH:

DATE:

LOCATION:

TIME:

TYPE:

HEIGHT:

DESCRIPTION:

SKETCH:

DATE:

LOCATION:

TIME:

TYPE:

HEIGHT:

DESCRIPTION:

SKETCH:

DATE:

LOCATION:

TIME:

TYPE:

HEIGHT:

DESCRIPTION:

SKETCH:

DATE:

LOCATION:

TIME:

TYPE:

HEIGHT:

DESCRIPTION:

SKETCH:

DATE:

LOCATION:

TIME:

TYPE:

HEIGHT:

DESCRIPTION:

SKETCH:

DATE:

LOCATION:

TIME:

TYPE:

HEIGHT:

DESCRIPTION:

SKETCH:

DATE:

LOCATION:

TIME:

TYPE:

HEIGHT:

DESCRIPTION:

SKETCH:

DATE:

LOCATION:

TIME:

TYPE:

HEIGHT:

DESCRIPTION:

SKETCH:

DATE:

LOCATION:

TIME:

TYPE:

HEIGHT:

DESCRIPTION:

SKETCH:

DATE:

LOCATION:

TIME:

TYPE:

HEIGHT:

DESCRIPTION:

SKETCH:

DATE:

LOCATION:

TIME:

TYPE:

HEIGHT:

DESCRIPTION:

SKETCH:

DATE:

LOCATION:

TIME:

TYPE:

HEIGHT:

DESCRIPTION:

SKETCH:

DATE:

LOCATION:

TIME:

TYPE:

HEIGHT:

DESCRIPTION:

SKETCH:

DATE:

LOCATION:

TIME:

TYPE:

HEIGHT:

DESCRIPTION:

SKETCH:

DATE:

LOCATION:

TIME:

TYPE:

HEIGHT:

DESCRIPTION:

SKETCH:

DATE:

LOCATION:

TIME:

TYPE:

HEIGHT:

DESCRIPTION:

SKETCH:

DATE:

LOCATION:

TIME:

TYPE:

HEIGHT:

DESCRIPTION:

SKETCH:

DATE:

LOCATION:

TIME:

TYPE:

HEIGHT:

DESCRIPTION:

SKETCH:

DATE:

LOCATION:

TIME:

TYPE:

HEIGHT:

DESCRIPTION:

SKETCH:

DATE:

LOCATION:

TIME:

TYPE:

HEIGHT:

DESCRIPTION:

SKETCH:

DATE:

LOCATION:

TIME:

TYPE:

HEIGHT:

DESCRIPTION:

SKETCH:

DATE:

LOCATION:

TIME:

TYPE:

HEIGHT:

DESCRIPTION:

SKETCH:

DATE:

LOCATION:

TIME:

TYPE:

HEIGHT:

DESCRIPTION:

SKETCH:

DATE:

LOCATION:

TIME:

TYPE:

HEIGHT:

DESCRIPTION:

SKETCH:

DATE:

LOCATION:

TIME:

TYPE:

HEIGHT:

DESCRIPTION:

SKETCH:

DATE:

LOCATION:

TIME:

TYPE:

HEIGHT:

DESCRIPTION:

SKETCH:

DATE:

LOCATION:

TIME:

TYPE:

HEIGHT:

DESCRIPTION:

SKETCH:

DATE:

LOCATION:

TIME:

TYPE:

HEIGHT:

DESCRIPTION:

SKETCH:

DATE:

LOCATION:

TIME:

TYPE:

HEIGHT:

DESCRIPTION:

SKETCH:

DATE:

LOCATION:

TIME:

TYPE:

HEIGHT:

DESCRIPTION:

SKETCH:

DATE:

LOCATION:

TIME:

TYPE:

HEIGHT:

DESCRIPTION:

SKETCH:

DATE:

LOCATION:

TIME:

TYPE:

HEIGHT:

DESCRIPTION:

SKETCH:

DATE:

LOCATION:

TIME:

TYPE:

HEIGHT:

DESCRIPTION:

SKETCH:

DATE:

LOCATION:

TIME:

TYPE:

HEIGHT:

DESCRIPTION:

SKETCH:

DATE:

LOCATION:

TIME:

TYPE:

HEIGHT:

DESCRIPTION:

SKETCH:

DATE:

LOCATION:

TIME:

TYPE:

HEIGHT:

DESCRIPTION:

SKETCH:

DATE:

LOCATION:

TIME:

TYPE:

HEIGHT:

DESCRIPTION:

SKETCH:

DATE:

LOCATION:

TIME:

TYPE:

HEIGHT:

DESCRIPTION:

SKETCH:

DATE:

LOCATION:

TIME:

TYPE:

HEIGHT:

DESCRIPTION:

SKETCH:

DATE:

LOCATION:

TIME:

TYPE:

HEIGHT:

DESCRIPTION:

SKETCH:

DATE:

LOCATION:

TIME:

TYPE:

HEIGHT:

DESCRIPTION:

SKETCH:

DATE:

LOCATION:

TIME:

TYPE:

HEIGHT:

DESCRIPTION:

SKETCH:

DATE:

LOCATION:

TIME:

TYPE:

HEIGHT:

DESCRIPTION:

SKETCH:

DATE:

LOCATION:

TIME:

TYPE:

HEIGHT:

DESCRIPTION:

SKETCH:

DATE:

LOCATION:

TIME:

TYPE:

HEIGHT:

DESCRIPTION:

SKETCH:

DATE:

LOCATION:

TIME:

TYPE:

HEIGHT:

DESCRIPTION:

SKETCH:

DATE:

LOCATION:

TIME:

TYPE:

HEIGHT:

DESCRIPTION:

SKETCH:

DATE:

LOCATION:

TIME:

TYPE:

HEIGHT:

DESCRIPTION:

SKETCH:

DATE:

LOCATION:

TIME:

TYPE:

HEIGHT:

DESCRIPTION:

SKETCH:

DATE:

LOCATION:

TIME:

TYPE:

HEIGHT:

DESCRIPTION:

SKETCH:

DATE:

LOCATION:

TIME:

TYPE:

HEIGHT:

DESCRIPTION:

SKETCH:

DATE:

LOCATION:

TIME:

TYPE:

HEIGHT:

DESCRIPTION:

SKETCH:

DATE:

LOCATION:

TIME:

TYPE:

HEIGHT:

DESCRIPTION:

SKETCH:

DATE:

LOCATION:

TIME:

TYPE:

HEIGHT:

DESCRIPTION:

SKETCH:

DATE:

LOCATION:

TIME:

TYPE:

HEIGHT:

DESCRIPTION:

SKETCH:

DATE:

LOCATION:

TIME:

TYPE:

HEIGHT:

DESCRIPTION:

SKETCH:

DATE:

LOCATION:

TIME:

TYPE:

HEIGHT:

DESCRIPTION:

SKETCH:

DATE:

LOCATION:

TIME:

TYPE:

HEIGHT:

DESCRIPTION:

SKETCH:

DATE:

LOCATION:

TIME:

TYPE:

HEIGHT:

DESCRIPTION:

SKETCH:

DATE:

LOCATION:

TIME:

TYPE:

HEIGHT:

DESCRIPTION:

SKETCH:

DATE:

LOCATION:

TIME:

TYPE:

HEIGHT:

DESCRIPTION:

SKETCH:

DATE:

LOCATION:

TIME:

TYPE:

HEIGHT:

DESCRIPTION:

SKETCH:

DATE:

LOCATION:

TIME:

TYPE:

HEIGHT:

DESCRIPTION:

SKETCH:

DATE:

LOCATION:

TIME:

TYPE:

HEIGHT:

DESCRIPTION:

SKETCH:

DATE:

LOCATION:

TIME:

TYPE:

HEIGHT:

DESCRIPTION:

SKETCH:

DATE:

LOCATION:

TIME:

TYPE:

HEIGHT:

DESCRIPTION:

SKETCH:

DATE:

LOCATION:

TIME:

TYPE:

HEIGHT:

DESCRIPTION:

SKETCH:

DATE:

LOCATION:

TIME:

TYPE:

HEIGHT:

DESCRIPTION:

SKETCH:

DATE:

LOCATION:

TIME:

TYPE:

HEIGHT:

DESCRIPTION:

SKETCH:

DATE:

LOCATION:

TIME:

TYPE:

HEIGHT:

DESCRIPTION:

SKETCH:

DATE:

LOCATION:

TIME:

TYPE:

HEIGHT:

DESCRIPTION:

SKETCH:

DATE:

LOCATION:

TIME:

TYPE:

HEIGHT:

DESCRIPTION:

SKETCH:

DATE:

LOCATION:

TIME:

TYPE:

HEIGHT:

DESCRIPTION:

SKETCH:

DATE:

LOCATION:

TIME:

TYPE:

HEIGHT:

DESCRIPTION:

SKETCH:

DATE:

LOCATION:

TIME:

TYPE:

HEIGHT:

DESCRIPTION:

SKETCH:

DATE:

LOCATION:

TIME:

TYPE:

HEIGHT:

DESCRIPTION:

SKETCH:

DATE:

LOCATION:

TIME:

TYPE:

HEIGHT:

DESCRIPTION:

SKETCH:

DATE:

LOCATION:

TIME:

TYPE:

HEIGHT:

DESCRIPTION:

SKETCH:

DATE:

LOCATION:

TIME:

TYPE:

HEIGHT:

DESCRIPTION:

SKETCH:

DATE:

LOCATION:

TIME:

TYPE:

HEIGHT:

DESCRIPTION:

SKETCH:

DATE:

LOCATION:

TIME:

TYPE:

HEIGHT:

DESCRIPTION:

SKETCH:

DATE:

LOCATION:

TIME:

TYPE:

HEIGHT:

DESCRIPTION:

SKETCH:

DATE:

LOCATION:

TIME:

TYPE:

HEIGHT:

DESCRIPTION:

SKETCH:

DATE:

LOCATION:

TIME:

TYPE:

HEIGHT:

DESCRIPTION:

SKETCH:

DATE:

LOCATION:

TIME:

TYPE:

HEIGHT:

DESCRIPTION:

SKETCH:

DATE:

LOCATION:

TIME:

TYPE:

HEIGHT:

DESCRIPTION:

SKETCH:

DATE:

LOCATION:

TIME:

TYPE:

HEIGHT:

DESCRIPTION:

SKETCH:

DATE:

LOCATION:

TIME:

TYPE:

HEIGHT:

DESCRIPTION:

SKETCH:

DATE:

LOCATION:

TIME:

TYPE:

HEIGHT:

DESCRIPTION:

SKETCH:

DATE:

LOCATION:

TIME:

TYPE:

HEIGHT:

DESCRIPTION:

SKETCH:

DATE:

LOCATION:

TIME:

TYPE:

HEIGHT:

DESCRIPTION:

SKETCH:

DATE:

LOCATION:

TIME:

TYPE:

HEIGHT:

DESCRIPTION:

SKETCH:

DATE:

LOCATION:

TIME:

TYPE:

HEIGHT:

DESCRIPTION:

SKETCH:

DATE:

LOCATION:

TIME:

TYPE:

HEIGHT:

DESCRIPTION:

SKETCH:

DATE:

LOCATION:

TIME:

TYPE:

HEIGHT:

DESCRIPTION:

SKETCH:

DATE:

LOCATION:

TIME:

TYPE:

HEIGHT:

DESCRIPTION:

SKETCH:

DATE:

LOCATION:

TIME:

TYPE:

HEIGHT:

DESCRIPTION:

SKETCH:

DATE:

LOCATION:

TIME:

TYPE:

HEIGHT:

DESCRIPTION:

SKETCH:

DATE:

LOCATION:

TIME:

TYPE:

HEIGHT:

DESCRIPTION:

SKETCH:

DATE:

LOCATION:

TIME:

TYPE:

HEIGHT:

DESCRIPTION:

SKETCH:

DATE:

LOCATION:

TIME:

TYPE:

HEIGHT:

DESCRIPTION:

SKETCH:

DATE:

LOCATION:

TIME:

TYPE:

HEIGHT:

DESCRIPTION:

SKETCH:

DATE:

LOCATION:

TIME:

TYPE:

HEIGHT:

DESCRIPTION:

SKETCH:

DATE:

LOCATION:

TIME:

TYPE:

HEIGHT:

DESCRIPTION:

SKETCH:

DATE:

LOCATION:

TIME:

TYPE:

HEIGHT:

DESCRIPTION:

SKETCH:

DATE:

LOCATION:

TIME:

TYPE:

HEIGHT:

DESCRIPTION:

SKETCH:

DATE:

LOCATION:

TIME:

TYPE:

HEIGHT:

DESCRIPTION:

SKETCH:

DATE:

LOCATION:

TIME:

TYPE:

HEIGHT:

DESCRIPTION:

SKETCH:

DATE:

LOCATION:

TIME:

TYPE:

HEIGHT:

DESCRIPTION:

SKETCH:

DATE:

LOCATION:

TIME:

TYPE:

HEIGHT:

DESCRIPTION:

SKETCH:

DATE:

LOCATION:

TIME:

TYPE:

HEIGHT:

DESCRIPTION:

SKETCH:

DATE:

LOCATION:

TIME:

TYPE:

HEIGHT:

DESCRIPTION:

SKETCH:

DATE:

LOCATION:

TIME:

TYPE:

HEIGHT:

DESCRIPTION:

SKETCH:

DATE:

LOCATION:

TIME:

TYPE:

HEIGHT:

DESCRIPTION:

SKETCH:

DATE:

LOCATION:

TIME:

TYPE:

HEIGHT:

DESCRIPTION:

SKETCH:

DATE:

LOCATION:

TIME:

TYPE:

HEIGHT:

DESCRIPTION:

SKETCH:

DATE:

LOCATION:

TIME:

TYPE:

HEIGHT:

DESCRIPTION:

SKETCH:

DATE:

LOCATION:

TIME:

TYPE:

HEIGHT:

DESCRIPTION:

SKETCH:

DATE:

LOCATION:

TIME:

TYPE:

HEIGHT:

DESCRIPTION:

SKETCH:

DATE:

LOCATION:

TIME:

TYPE:

HEIGHT:

DESCRIPTION:

SKETCH:

DATE:

LOCATION:

TIME:

TYPE:

HEIGHT:

DESCRIPTION:

SKETCH:

DATE:

LOCATION:

TIME:

TYPE:

HEIGHT:

DESCRIPTION:

SKETCH:

DATE:

LOCATION:

TIME:

TYPE:

HEIGHT:

DESCRIPTION:

SKETCH:

DATE:

LOCATION:

TIME:

TYPE:

HEIGHT:

DESCRIPTION:

SKETCH:

DATE:

LOCATION:

TIME:

TYPE:

HEIGHT:

DESCRIPTION:

SKETCH:

DATE:

LOCATION:

TIME:

TYPE:

HEIGHT:

DESCRIPTION:

SKETCH:

DATE:

LOCATION:

TIME:

TYPE:

HEIGHT:

DESCRIPTION:

SKETCH:

DATE:

LOCATION:

TIME:

TYPE:

HEIGHT:

DESCRIPTION:

SKETCH:

DATE:

LOCATION:

TIME:

TYPE:

HEIGHT:

DESCRIPTION:

SKETCH:

DATE:

LOCATION:

TIME:

TYPE:

HEIGHT:

DESCRIPTION:

SKETCH:

DATE:

LOCATION:

TIME:

TYPE:

HEIGHT:

DESCRIPTION:

SKETCH:

DATE:

LOCATION:

TIME:

TYPE:

HEIGHT:

DESCRIPTION:

SKETCH:

DATE:

LOCATION:

TIME:

TYPE:

HEIGHT:

DESCRIPTION:

SKETCH:

DATE:

LOCATION:

TIME:

TYPE:

HEIGHT:

DESCRIPTION:

SKETCH:

DATE:

LOCATION:

TIME:

TYPE:

HEIGHT:

DESCRIPTION:

SKETCH:

DATE:

LOCATION:

TIME:

TYPE:

HEIGHT:

DESCRIPTION:

SKETCH:

DATE:

LOCATION:

TIME:

TYPE:

HEIGHT:

DESCRIPTION:

SKETCH:

DATE:

LOCATION:

TIME:

TYPE:

HEIGHT:

DESCRIPTION:

SKETCH:

DATE:

LOCATION:

TIME:

TYPE:

HEIGHT:

DESCRIPTION:

SKETCH:

DATE:

LOCATION:

TIME:

TYPE:

HEIGHT:

DESCRIPTION:

SKETCH:

DATE:

LOCATION:

TIME:

TYPE:

HEIGHT:

DESCRIPTION:

SKETCH:

DATE:

LOCATION:

TIME:

TYPE:

HEIGHT:

DESCRIPTION:

SKETCH:

DATE:

LOCATION:

TIME:

TYPE:

HEIGHT:

DESCRIPTION:

SKETCH:

DATE:

LOCATION:

TIME:

TYPE:

HEIGHT:

DESCRIPTION:

SKETCH:

DATE:

LOCATION:

TIME:

TYPE:

HEIGHT:

DESCRIPTION:

SKETCH:

DATE:

LOCATION:

TIME:

TYPE:

HEIGHT:

DESCRIPTION:

SKETCH:

DATE:

LOCATION:

TIME:

TYPE:

HEIGHT:

DESCRIPTION:

SKETCH:

DATE:

LOCATION:

TIME:

TYPE:

HEIGHT:

DESCRIPTION:

SKETCH:

DATE:

LOCATION:

TIME:

TYPE:

HEIGHT:

DESCRIPTION:

SKETCH:

DATE:

LOCATION:

TIME:

TYPE:

HEIGHT:

DESCRIPTION:

SKETCH:

DATE:

LOCATION:

TIME:

TYPE:

HEIGHT:

DESCRIPTION:

SKETCH:

DATE:

LOCATION:

TIME:

TYPE:

HEIGHT:

DESCRIPTION:

SKETCH:

DATE:

LOCATION:

TIME:

TYPE:

HEIGHT:

DESCRIPTION:

SKETCH:

DATE:

LOCATION:

TIME:

TYPE:

HEIGHT:

DESCRIPTION:

SKETCH:

DATE:

LOCATION:

TIME:

TYPE:

HEIGHT:

DESCRIPTION:

SKETCH:

DATE:

LOCATION:

TIME:

TYPE:

HEIGHT:

DESCRIPTION:

SKETCH:

DATE:

LOCATION:

TIME:

TYPE:

HEIGHT:

DESCRIPTION:

SKETCH:

DATE:

LOCATION:

TIME:

TYPE:

HEIGHT:

DESCRIPTION:

SKETCH:

DATE:

LOCATION:

TIME:

TYPE:

HEIGHT:

DESCRIPTION:

SKETCH:

aJournals

2019

aJournals

Tempelhofer Ufer 15
10963 Berlin
Germany

53316588R00120

Made in the USA
Middletown, DE
11 July 2019